Walter Malone

Songs of December & June

Walter Malone

Songs of December & June

ISBN/EAN: 9783337181413

Printed in Europe, USA, Canada, Australia, Japan

Cover: Foto ©Thomas Meinert / pixelio.de

More available books at **www.hansebooks.com**

SONGS OF DECEMBER & JUNE

BY

WALTER MALONE

AUTHOR OF "SONGS
OF DUSK AND DAWN"

PHILADELPHIA
PRINTED BY J. B. LIPPINCOTT COMPANY
1896

TO

HENRY F. WALSH

I INSCRIBE

THIS VOLUME.

CONTENTS.

	PAGE
THE ORIOLE	7
THE BLUEBIRD	12
THE PENITENTIARY	18
THE HUMBLER POETS	24
CAPELLA	26
THE MOON FLOWER	28
THE POPPY	30
THE CHRYSANTHEMUM	32
MY FIRST BOOK	33
THE POET TO HIS BOOK	34
MY BRIDE	37
"WHEN I HAVE LOST YOU"	39
THE QUEEN OF THE VALENTINES	42
KATHARINE	45
A SUMMER NIGHT	46
RENAN'S LIFE OF JESUS	48
BELLINI	50
THE CRY OF A DEBTOR	52
NAPOLEON AND BYRON	54
"BLESSED ARE THE DEAD WHO DIE IN THE LORD"	55

5

SONGS OF
DECEMBER & JUNE.

___

THE ORIOLE.

I.

Oriole, swift oriole,
All the Orient glories stole
In the splendor of your sable and your orange plumes,
Come from tropic lands of fire
In your royal, rich attire,
Like the dazzle of a dawning through the ebon mid-
    night glooms.

Oriole, swift oriole,
Like a fiery-hearted coal,
Or a blazing topaz in the darkness of a mine,
Like a blossom black as night
With a breast of burning light,
Or the jet and saffron banners of an autumn day's
    decline.

Like a meteor's yellow spark
In the bosom of the dark,
Like the flaming treasures of the old Arabian caves,

Like the gems a gypsy wears,
Tiger eyes in lurid lairs,
Or a crown of flashing jewels in a dead king's gloomy
    grave.

Oriole, swift oriole,
Like the fierce and fiery soul
Of a blasted angel who is doomed for evermore,
Come from tropic lands of light
Unto Northern lands of night
Over palms of peerless islands, over ocean's sullen roar !

Oriole, swift oriole,
You are like a shining scroll,
All the tropic glories burnished in your brilliant wings,
And our tender Northern blooms
Waken from their chilly tombs
As you flame above our forests in the summers and the
    springs.

II.

In the ages that have fled,
In the generations dead,
Far away in richest regions of the Southern land,
You were eldest son and heir
To a proud king ruling there,
Dwelling at a peerless palace, rising in a garden grand.

But one day it came to pass
That you loved a beggar lass
In this Northern land of storm and shadow far away,

In this land of gloom and grief,
Wailing wind and autumn leaf,
Where the queenly summers perish in October skies of
    gray ;

In this land of want and woe,
In this land of sleet and snow,
Where the sad September glimmers through a mist of
    tears,
Where the birds are poor and plain,
And the blossoms all are slain
When the dark December conquers all the kingdoms
    of the years.

And the beggar maiden thrush
All her silvery songs would hush
If she heard your footsteps coming to her secret
    nest,
For your love the lass returned,
And her fervent bosom burned,
And her tender heart would flutter with a sweet and
    sad unrest.

But they tore you two apart,
Prisoned you with aching heart
Far away beyond the trackless oceans of the South,
Leaving her to pine alone,
With the winter winds to moan,
And your kisses fell no longer on her eager, upturned
    mouth.

But you prayed and pleaded so,
In your loneliness and woe,
That they let you come to see her as the springtime
    came,
And you lingered by her side,
Through the golden Summer tide,
Till the mournful Autumn shattered all her palaces of
    flame.

And you come to see her still
When the springtime bowers thrill,
When the gorgeous summer blossoms on the hill-tops
    blaze,
When the water-lily blows,
And the trumpet-flower glows,
And the golden August harvests glimmer in a mellow
    maze.

From the South you flutter forth
To the grim and gloomy North,
And you bring the fiery splendors of the tropic
    noons,
Bringing dreams of plumy palms,
Bringing dreams of slumbering calms,
Where the everlasting summer in delicious languor
    swoons.

But when autumn showers come,
And the blossoms all are numb,
You must leave the little maiden, whom you love, alone,

When the winds of Winter blow,
And the fields are filled with snow,
She must wander, broken-hearted, as the bitter tempests
    moan.

Oriole, swift oriole,
So it was with mine own soul
When the One Love came to greet me with his flags of
    fire ;
All was piercing, burning bliss,
Life was like a clinging kiss,
And my breast was palpitating with a sweet and strange
    desire.

Love has brought me days of dole ;
Love my peace and quiet stole
When he came with fierce embraces from the fervent
    South,
When he came from fabled lands,
And he pressed my trembling hands,
And I felt the honeyed kisses from his passion-pulsing
    mouth.

Oriole, swift oriole,
Like a black and smouldering coal
Is my heart, that once was burning with a golden glow,
And the fields of lambent light
Now are hid in solemn night,
And my summer's tropic splendors shrouded in Decem-
    ber snow.

THE BLUEBIRD.

WHEN the bluebird comes in the days of spring,
With a sweet, soft note and a swift, wild wing,
When the redbuds blush and the dogwoods bloom,
And the marigold comes from her chilly tomb,

When the fox-glove peers through the tender grass,
And the bluet peeps like a roguish lass,
When the South winds rush with a swirl of showers,
And a bugle blast through the budding bowers,

Then I hear the moan and the pensive plaint
Of his throbbing throat, like a love-song faint
From the far, far lands where the dear ones go
When they leave us lorn in a world of woe.

So the primrose knows of his secret well,
And the brown bee learns from the lily bell,
And the wrens have heard from the friendly doves
That the violet sweet is the one he loves.

And they say his heart is forever true
To the one wee maid with the eyes of blue;
At his songs she wakes in the morning light,
And they fold her lids at the fall of night.

12

In the days of old, so the wild flowers say,
When the world was young as an April day,
When the red man roved through the Western wild
With a heart as free as a wilful child,

Then the bluebird came as an angel white
From the lands of love and the lands of light,
Where the blasts never blow and the skies never
 snow,
And he trod with men through the world below,

Till his eyes were cast on the damsel sweet,
With her flower-like face and her fawn-like feet,
And they loved so well that the birds and bees
Would repeat the tale to the gossiping trees.

Of a mortal race was the lovely maid,
And the day would dawn when her face would fade,
While the angel came from a world on high,
Where the night falls not, nor the blest ones die.

In her youth and joy was the sharp shaft sped,
And they laid her low with the dreamless dead ;
So she passed away from her consort brave,
And his clasp and kiss to the silent grave.

So the fleet days fly and the years pass by,
And the centuries fade and the ages die,
And he pines away in his passion true
Till his raiment white is an ashen blue.

So the bluebird sings to his long-lost love
Through the fields below and the skies above,
From the noon to night, through the misty morn,
Through the summers, the springs, and the falls forlorn.

And she loves him so as he pours his notes,
And the dear, dear call through the forest floats
In her moulded shroud, after long, long years,
She awakes at last and her loved one hears.

When the springtime comes through the sleet and snow,
And she hears his voice in her grave below,
She returns to him with her dear, dark eyes,
And a violet blooms under April skies.

But the bluebird sings, and her lips are dumb,
And the bluebird calls, but she cannot come,
And the one reply she makes from her tomb
Is her soft, soft breath, with its frail perfume.

When he sings love-songs she but sobs and sighs,
And her sweet, sweet breath in its dumbness dies;
As the dew-drops fall she is faint with fears,
And her blue, blue eyes are bedimmed with tears.

But the wild flowers hear what the lovers say
Through the ardent hours of the sweet spring day;
They have told the words of their songs to me,
And so I will tell of their secrets to thee.

THE BLUEBIRD.

"Violet sweet, with the eyes of blue,
Violet sweet, with the diadem dew,
Violet sweet, the dearest to me,
Violet sweet, I am waiting for thee!

"Lying alone in thy dungeon gloom,
Parted from me in thy mournful tomb,
Sleeping, O love, with a heart of lead,
Listen to me, and wake from the dead!

"Violet sweet, I am filled with fears,
Violet sweet, I am blind with tears,
Violet sweet, awake to my trill,
Violet sweet, I am faithful still!"

THE VIOLET.

"Beautiful bird, I have waited long,
Beautiful bird, I have heard thy song,
Beautiful bird, so faithful to me,
Beautiful bird, I love none but thee!

"Waiting for years under dank, dark sods,
Shrouded and still under hard, cold clods,
Numb with despair, my hopes had all fled,
Loveless, alone with the dreamless dead.

"Beautiful bird, bringing life unto me,
Beautiful bird, I am coming to thee,
Beautiful bird, from death I depart,
Beautiful bird, to thy sweet, sweet heart!"

THE BLUEBIRD.

" Loving thee still when the mock-birds call,
  Loving thee still when the red leaves fall,
  Loving thee still when the blue-bell blows,
  Loving thee still through the chill, white snows ;

" Loving thee still in the radiant noons,
  Loving thee still under ghostly moons,
  Loving thee still as the days go by,
  Loving thee still as the dim years die.''

THE VIOLET.

" Dreaming of thee in the bleak, black earth,
  Dreaming of thee in the dim, dark dearth,
  Dreaming of thee in the morning light,
  Dreaming of thee in the mournful night ;

" Dreaming of thee through the winter gloom,
  Dreaming of thee through the springtime bloom,
  Dreaming of thee as I ope to the sky,
  Dreaming of thee as I wither and die.''

THE BLUEBIRD.

" And the wild rose singeth her songs to me,
  Seeking, O precious, to woo me from thee,
  And her proud head bends from her stately seat
  In scorn upon thee far down at her feet ;

" The marsh lily sayeth she is fairer by far,
  With her white, white breast, her face like a star,

She begs me, O sweet, to flee from thy side
And make her, O sweet, my love and my bride.

" But never shall I grow faithless to thee,
  O fairest and sweetest and truest to me !
  My heart and my soul forever are wed
  To the one lost love in realms of the dead."

THE PENITENTIARY.

I.

I SEE the convicts in disgraceful stripes
  Come homeward to their cells at set of sun,
The whole world's most despised, disgusting types,
  As hopeless as the day that now is done.

The penitentiary opens iron jaws
  To swallow up the mass of shame and sin,
The cages seize them in their rusty claws,
  And giant gates are locked to keep them in.

Their faces all are foul, their hands unclean,
  Their aching ankles drag the iron ball,
And two by two they bear a clanking chain;
  Their heads are shaved to show their hopeless fall.

One sings lewd songs, one tells a wicked jest,
  They laugh at Honor and they laugh at Shame;
All that on Earth is sweetest and is best
  Is scoffed and blasphemed with a vulgar name.

Here comes a man who sought to make escape;
  Behold the swollen stripes of whip and rod!—
What shame to think that one in mortal shape
  Should beat and spit upon a child of God!

18

I pity them and feel a rush of tears,
  But not one creature here has tears to shed,
For they have never sobbed since childhood years,
  As all their hopes and loves and joys are dead.

And then my heart is hardened as I hear
  How every virtue from their souls is driven ;
I shrink and shudder as they come too near,
  Exiled from Earth and hurled from hopes of Heaven !

II.

And yet I feel all good is not yet lost ;
  This man would share with me his crust of bread,
Would bring me water when with fever tost,
  Or share with me his narrow iron bed.

Or, if I told him some sweet tale of love,
  A smile would light his face's dull despair,
As lovely as the white wings of a dove
  Amid the darkness of a panther's lair.

Once more a tender touch his heart would feel
  To think of one he loved in years of yore,
Before the Law came, with its chains of steel,
  And bade him banish hope for evermore.

Or, if I travelled through a lonely land,
  In storms of midnight, when my feet grew sore,
Were he a hermit, he would take my hand
  And give me gracious welcome to his door.

Or, if a slave, I hid from haunts of men,
　Or fled in terror from pursuing hounds,
This thief would lead me safely to his den,
　And pour the oil upon my burning wounds.

If this be true of this poor convict now,
　How far, far happier might have been his fate
If chance temptation had not warped his brow,
　And friendly warning had not come too late!

And there are thousands in the world to-day
　Who never will be called to answer crimes,
Enthroned in wealth, to rule with despot sway,
　Though viler than these clods a hundred times.

The shivering wretch who steals a tattered coat
　Or crust to keep his starving soul alive,
A rusty penny, or a cankered groat,—
　That is the thief the world will not forgive.

But he who blights a maiden in her bud,
　Who snatches gold by force, or fraud, or might,
And he who bathes a nation in its blood,
　Walks forth as free as Heaven's own air and light.

Here treads a generous spendthrift, who at last,
　In evil moment, like a culprit fell;
His fawners and his flatterers of the past,
　All, all have left him in a convict's cell;

And, as he treads in felon's stripes and chains,
  He learns the story told from sun to sun,—
Be generous; and men mock you for your pains;
  Be selfish; and your crown is surely won.

Here comes a poor old drunkard, weak and worn,
  His face all bloated, dark with leaden care,
His ashen eyes, once clear as skies of morn,
  Are dim and dull with unexpressed despair;

While he who held the bottle to his lips,
  Who robbed him of his last poor coin at play,
And she whose sweet lies made his soul's eclipse,
  Are roving free and happy far away.

Here comes a woman who was pure and young,
  A lily that was trampled in the dust,
Whose lover's treason like an adder stung,—
  Another victim to a foolish trust;

But while she pines in penitentiary walls
  Her false seducer cares not for her doom;
He treads his measures in his gilded halls,
  She in the treadmill of this living tomb;

And she shall kiss no more the roses red,
  And in her youth and sweetness laugh aloud;
A felon's couch shall be her bridal bed,
  A wreath of fennel rest upon her shroud.

But though the world may not believe me just,
　I pardon him who steals a loaf of bread,
But not the wretch who breaks my tender trust,
　And leaves me with an aching heart of lead.

My soul forgives that poor old drunken man,
　That outcast, shivering through the cruel town,
But not the chieftain of a robber clan,
　Who steals my freedom and who wears a crown.

But then the world is strong and I am weak;
　You are the creatures of the powers that be;
So you must fester in your dungeons bleak
　Till Death shall come at last to set you free.

III.

But midnight comes; each on a bed of straw,
　I see the two men and the woman lie;
Their servitude has satisfied the law,
　For now the hour of death is drawing nigh.

Their fevered brains are swayed by fitful dreams,
　Their dim eyes glance through scenes of perished
　　years,
And sweet, sad visions come in hazy gleams
　Beyond the realm of sin and shame and tears.

And they remember, in a broken prayer,
　With deaf, dull ears and dim and dying eyes,
How Christ once calmed the dying thief's despair,
　" To-day thou meetest me in Paradise."

Who is this stranger treading by to night,
    A stranger coming from the far, far lands,
His sad face lovely with a smile of light,
    Who bears the prints of nails upon his hands?

" Behold, ye dying sinners ! wake, arise !
    Ho, turnkey, jailer, open unto me !
For we shall meet to-night in Paradise,
    The King of Heaven Himself has pardoned ye !

" Behold, ye dying sinners ! wake, arise !
    Ho, turnkey, jailer, open unto me !
The convict in his straw-strewn dungeon dies,
    For Christ Himself has come to set him free !"

THE HUMBLER POETS.

THE critic wonders why the humbler bards
  Still write and write when no one seems to read,
When fame and fortune still refuse rewards,
  And when the world gives but a wreath of weed.

But still, Sir Critic, they have done their best,
  And more than that not Shakespeare's self has done;
For while God gave ten talents to the rest,
  To these poor poets He has given but one.

And if a lowly singer dries one tear,
  Or soothes one humble human heart in pain,
Be sure his homely verse to God is dear,
  And not one stanza has been sung in vain.

So when they give their humble songs of praise,
  Their simple lines find favor in His sight,
And when He loves to hear their little lays,
  Rebuke not, for His spirit saith " Write !"

They do not come as kings and queens of song,
  Surrounded by the pomp of spears and shields,
But patient peasants, suffering scorn and wrong,
  To labor in His vineyards and His fields.

24

Theirs not the strains of thrushes' golden throats
   That haunt the soul with visions of delight,
Nor peerless mock-birds' palpitating notes,
   That thrill the morning and the noon and night;

But like the robins, with their hopeful trill,
   They bring first tidings of the coming spring,
Or, like brown snow-birds in the winter chill,
   They cheer us when their brothers will not sing.

They come not like the roses, winged with fire,
   In scarfs of scarlet or in gowns of gold,
Nor like the lilies, decked in white attire,
   Whose leaflets like a seraph's plumes unfold;

But, like wild cowslips, fresh from nature's woof,
   That make a poet of a farmer boy,
Or daisies on a dusty city roof,
   That give a poor, sick working-woman joy.

Then sing on, humble poet! God will hear,
   And He will praise you for your work well done;
Then, when you see Him, you may find no peer
   Among the throngs that sing around His throne.

CAPELLA.

AMID the solemn shadows of the night
    I see Capella, star of stars, arise,
In everlasting splendor, pure and white,
    The peerless diamond of the Northern skies.

Night after night I see her rise again,
    Immortal, ever young and ever proud,
An empress born for evermore to reign,
    To shine upon my cradle and my shroud.

She sees me when, a halcyon-hearted boy,
    I tread through dewy buds in morning years ;
She sees old age my royal hopes destroy,
    And sees my gray head bent with toils and tears.

She sees my heart's own darling, young and gay,
    And sees her fondly treading by my side ;
She sees her taken from me far away
    Beyond the mountains and the oceans wide.

She sees the mighty monarchs in their mirth,
    And sees their sceptres redden into rust ;
She sees the haughty empires at their birth,
    And sees their ruins crumble into dust.

26

But when our skies are flecked with autumn leaves,
    Or with the fluttering flakes of winter snows,
When earth above her dying millions grieves,
    And sobs and sobs amid her myriad woes;

In that far island of immortal light
    Imperial summer lingers evermore,
A land of lilies, robed in spotless white,
    Beyond the earthquake and the ocean roar;

And there the great gods in their banquet halls
    With wreaths of roses deck their golden hair,
No flower fades, no autumn leaflet falls,
    And joy is never shadowed by despair.

And there within their marble palaces
    They quaff the purple and the golden wine,
And, gazing in the crystal chalices,
    Forget our woes amid their bliss divine.

THE MOON FLOWER.

I see the splendor of thy blooms of white,
  Spotless and stainless in thine innocence,
Adorning solemn shadows of the night,
  Unnoticed in thy lone magnificence.

Not like the gorgeous blossoms of the morn,
  In princely purple or in royal red,
Amid the glories of the sunrise born,
  To wither when their lover, Dawn, lies dead;

Nor like thy radiant sisters of the noon,
  With burning bosoms blushing in the sun,
Whose fierce embraces make them sway and swoon,
  Until they perish as the day is done;

For they have felt their fervent love returned,
  And all the ardor of a clasp and kiss,
Have palpitated and have thrilled and burned
  With sweet delirium of the lover's bliss;

While thou, pale virgin, pinest all alone,
  A shrouded star, in ghostly robes of white,
No lover's kiss thy pearl-pure face hath known
  To make thee pant with passionate delight.

28

No brown bee ever comes to taste thy lips,
　No bird will ever sing his songs to thee,
No sunbeam steals to touch thy tingling tips,
　Thy maiden charms no bridal day shall see.

And yet, O peerless, pearly, pure moon flower,
　Thy sweet mouth trembles with a strange perfume,
And thou dost make a heaven of thy bower
　Though no true lover comes to cheer thy doom.

And so thy tale of love is never told,
　Thy secret dieth with the morning light,
Though virgin bosoms throb, we call thee cold,
　And see thee die in barrenness and blight.

And so True Love amid the darkness blooms,
　In silence, desolation—all alone,
With snow-white splendor lost in mournful glooms,
　And lives and dies unnoticed and unknown.

3*

THE POPPY.

Beside the pathway, as I tread along,
  I see the poppy, flushed with fierce desire,
Her hot breath like a passion-panting song,
  A scarlet siren with a heart of fire.

She tempts the traveller with her wicked wiles
  To sweet, delicious slumber in her snare,
To snatch lewd kisses and to share her smiles,
  And revel in the raptures of her lair.

She offers him her red, voluptuous mouth,
  Her bright head bending like a serpent's crest,
Her sighs like fierce siroccos of the South
  Above the billows of her burning breast.

She grasps him in her swoonful, sinful arms,
  And hides her lover in her shining hair ;
She smites him with the splendor of her charms,
  And blinds him with her secret sweets laid bare.

And soon her captive learns to love her so
  That he will glory in her sin and shame ;
He throws the world away to share her woe,
  And madly rushes to her bed of flame.
  30

He then forgets the loved ones of the past,
  The fame and fortune that he sought of yore,
His pride and honor in the dust are cast,
  And all his hopes are slain for evermore.

And so I fancy ages long ago,
  When thou wert young and sweet and full of grace,
Some son of man seduced thee, wrought thy woe,
  And thou hast sworn to wreck his hateful race.

So thou, O poppy, flamest by my path,
  In all thy scarlet splendor, fierce and fell,
To flaunt high heaven in its righteous wrath,
  Handmaid of Satan, harlot queen of Hell.

THE CHRYSANTHEMUM.

CHRYSANTHEMUM, chrysanthemum,
When autumn winds are numb,
When jasmines all have fled,
And pansies all are dead,
I see your gorgeous robes unfold,
In crimson and in purple and in gold.

Chrysanthemum, chrysanthemum,
When all the birds are dumb,
When leafless boughs are chill,
And summer insects still,
I feel your passionate perfume,
A fervid sweetness in this lonesome gloom.

Chyrsanthemum, chrysanthemum,
So shall the poet come;
Through shattered spring-time bowers,
Through chill November showers,
To rear his kingdom in the frost,
Consoling men for summers that are lost.

MY FIRST BOOK.

Poor little volume, awkward, rough and crude,
   Now soiled and battered like a tarnished toy !
   Yet thou wert once my childhood's pride and joy
Before contemptuous critics might intrude ;
And so I treasure still thy verses rude,
   As some poor mother loves her first-born boy,
   Who comes deformed, her high hopes to destroy,
And fill her breast with sad solicitude.

Still, I was happy in those perished years,
   Ere Sin had lured me onward to her snare,
While now my soul is racked with fitful fears,
   And Sorrow makes my gloomy heart her lair.
O for thy childish joys to dry my tears,
Thy childish hopes to soothe my dark despair !

THE POET TO HIS BOOK.

I SEND thee forth upon an unknown sea,
  Where many a bark hath perished long before;
In thee, my ship, I put the heart of me,
  To sail or sink from sight for evermore.

My treasures all are there like silken bales,
  Ambitions, aspirations, fancies, fears,
And in thy cargo, under snowy sails,
  Are all my joys and smiles and hopes and tears.

I see thy white breast, like a stately swan,
  Go forth to brave the wild waves of the deep,
When summer skies are rosy with the dawn
  And all the coming tempests are asleep.

God grant thee strength to live through stormy shocks,
  God guide thee ever under summer skies,
And send thee safely by the reefs and rocks
  To ever-blooming isles of Paradise.

Mayhap thy verse in ages yet to come
  Shall tell my secrets unto alien ears,
When this weak tongue hath lain for ages dumb
  And I have mouldered for a thousand years;

34

When she to whom in vain my love is told
  No longer reigns a Princess young and proud,
When clods have covered all her locks of gold
  And starry eyes are hidden in her shroud.

And then perchance when all our tribes have fled,
  When all the sceptres of the earth are rust,
When all the kingdoms of our day are dead,
  And all our cities crumbled into dust ;

When other nations with another tongue
  Have overcome the nations of to-day,
And heroes now unknown are praised and sung,
  And unborn poets hold the world in sway ;

When islets of the Australasian seas
  Have stolen Europe's light and Europe's soul,
And when the traveller knows all mysteries,
  From Afric jungle to the Northern pole ;

When crumbling idols, wreathed with weeds and
     vines,
  Gaze from the ruined temples of to day,
When strange, new gods are throned in other shrines
  And all our earth and heaven have passed away ;—

Then may my thoughts in others live again,
  A million bosoms may my transports share,
A million friends may feel my joy and pain,
  A million lovers feel my deep despair ;

And gentle maids may give me soulful sighs
  For true love offered that was not returned,
May hearken to my fervent melodies,
  And sob at learning how my bosom burned;

And I will tell to all the sons of men
  How fair the maiden whom I now adore,
And they shall hearken to my story then,
  And learn how I grew sad for evermore;

And they shall know my hours of loneliness,
  My true heart's anguish and unheeded sighs,
And how she slew my hopes of happiness
  With daggers of her splendor-streaming eyes.

MY BRIDE.

I SEE thee coming robed in spotless white,
   My stately swan, my pure and peerless dove,
My star of morning, diademed with light,
   Bringing me lilies from the lands of love.

I see a misty veil around thee float,
   As fragile as a dream, O bride so fair!
Wearing pale roses at thy pearly throat,
   And orange-blossoms in thy shining hair.

As lovely as the maiden moon in May,
   Above the lilacs where the lovers meet,
With spring-time songsters warbling in thy way,
   And all the summer flowers at thy feet.

The dawn is rising like a rosy boy,
   Running before thee, strewing garlands green,
Thy pretty page, with tidings full of joy,
   Bride of my soul, my princess and my queen!

Yet something tells me thou wilt never come,
   No bridal day mine eyes shall ever see,
That I must wait until my heart grows numb,
   Longing forever, precious love, for thee.

I dream I see thee in the spirit lands,
    With wan moon flowers in thy wreath of white,
A radiant star-like cereus in thy hands,
    The ghostly empress of the blooms of night;

I see the pale daturas in that waste,
    Sick with the sweetness of their poisoned breath,
And I behold thee, in thy beauty chaste,
    Treading alone, to be the bride of Death.

But oh, my sweet, I fear another doom,
    More than the coffin, shroud, and burial stone,—
That, ere we two are laid within the tomb,
    Another, sweet, shall claim thee for his own.

Though I am so unworthy, precious bride,
    And though his soul is not so dark as mine,
I cannot bear to see thee by his side,
    I cannot bear to hear thee call him thine.

Forgive, forgive this selfish, selfish heart
    That shudders as it dreams of thee as dead,
Yet prays and prays, if we are torn apart,
    That thou, like me, be evermore unwed!

"WHEN I HAVE LOST YOU."

When I have lost you, sweet, for evermore,
  When others, whom you trust not, come to woo,
Will you be happy as in years of yore,
  Or will you find a lover half so true?

False loves may dazzle with deceitful bloom,
  Heartless and soulless, on capricious wing,
Like gaudy tropic flowers without perfume,
  Or gaudy tropic birds that never sing;

But you may long to see my dead heart rise
  To tell its story of unheeded throes,
When autumn fades the splendor of your eyes
  And bright brown tresses all are flecked with snows.

I wonder if your heart will ache for me
  When one less kind shall claim you for his own;
If you will long my loving face to see
  When others leave you, dear, to weep alone;

If you will miss me in your distant home,
  And long to see me sitting by your side,
Then hear another's careless footstep come—
  Your loveless master—weal or woe betide?

No longer shall I tread with footsteps free
   Through flowery fields that knew me when a boy,
And hear the brooks and breezes sing to me,
   To thrill me with the story of their joy;

No longer shall I heed the summer skies,
   The rose of dawn, the lily of the noon,
The splendid sunset's iridescent dyes,
   The golden blossom of the rising moon.

And then my heart, a captive evermore,
   Shall linger, like a bird of paradise
Shut in a cage upon a Northern shore,
   With drooping plumage and with faded eyes.

He gazes out upon the dusty town,
   And hears the endless tread of restless feet,
Surrounded by the dingy roofs of brown
   And the dull thunder of the city street.

And when the autumn strews her withered leaves,
   And drear December scatters down his snows,
For vanished tropic splendors still he grieves
   Where spring-time, like a fadeless blossom, blows;

He longs once more to see the plumy palms,
   The vines, with clustered fruitage drooping low,
The tangled wilderness of blooms and balms,
   The seas of sapphire and the peaks of snow.

And then he yearns to see his mate again,
   Far, far away in forests of the South,
To tell her of his long, long years of pain,
   And woo her, breast to breast and mouth to mouth ;

But still he feels he is forgotten there,
   And long ago she chose another mate,
Forgetful of his faithful heart's despair,
   So, if set free, his call would come too late.

4*

THE QUEEN OF THE VALENTINES.

I.

" LITTLE bird, little bird, coming back from the South,
    Where spring-time's youth never dies,
With a melody sweet in your passionate mouth
    To gladden our gloomy skies;

" Little bird, little bird, in the days long ago,
    A prince you lived and you died,
And you flit like a leaf through the sun and the snow,
    Over earth and ocean wide.

" You have seen in the days that forever have fled
    Full many a fair, fair face,
And to-day you behold merry maidens that tread
    With gladsomest fawn-like grace;

" Will you say, little bird, if you've seen in your flight
    A maiden as fair as mine;
With a smile half as sweet, with a step half as light,
    Or eyes, like her own, divine?"

II.

" Never, O never, in sunshine or shadow,
    Never, O never, on mountain or meadow,
    Never, O never, in legends of glory,
    Never, O never, in song or in story,

" On the glad, green earth or the ocean wide,
    Has a maiden lived or a maiden died,
    In the huts below or the halls above,
    As sweet as the sweet, sweet maid you love.

" There were proud, proud queens in the days of old,
    With their white, white brows and their locks of gold,
    So stately and tall, so witchingly sweet,
    That the heroes died at their lovely feet ;

" There were maids beloved by the bards of yore,
    Whose beauty is treasured for evermore
    In the songs still sung as the bards sung then,
    And ever shall be by the sons of men ;

" Though the heart regrets, and the memory lingers
    On the vanished queens and sweethearts of singers,
    O lover, O lover, the maiden thou greetest
    Is fairest of all,. and brightest and sweetest.''

III.

All things that are fair at night and at noon
    Are blent in the face of my sweet,
From the stately orb of the full white moon
    To the bluebell low at her feet ;

From the diamond crown of the evening star
    To the dew on the pansy's plume,
From the blush in cheeks of the dawn afar
    To the blush on the peach-tree's bloom.

Fairer than them all in the ages fled,
   In the banished or vanished scenes,
Than roses living or the lilies dead,
   Sweetest of sweethearts, queen of queens !

KATHARINE.

A POEM thou wouldst have me write to thee,
  But words are all too weak and rhymes too dull
To bear the message from the heart of me,
  O maiden, blithest and most beautiful,

Though I should warble melting melodies
  As sweet as singing of a dying swan
Who floats with white wings under roseate skies
  To perish in the splendors of the dawn;

I find a romance in thy gladsome grace,
  Love-stories in the mazes of thy hair,
A peerless poem in thy fair young face,
  And in thy soul a song beyond compare,

A lover's lute-strings in thy laughter sweet,
  With strains of seraphs in thy gentle sighs,
A lilting lyric in thy footsteps fleet,
  And tragic splendor in thy sparkling eyes.

A SUMMER NIGHT.

Do you remember how the moon arose that summer
    night,
And how it bathed the jasmines in its mellow golden
    light?
Do you remember how the mock-bird twittered in his
    tree,
And how the whole world seemed a paradise to you
    and me?

Do you remember how the lilies, diademed with dew,
Seemed like a host of white-robed bridesmaids, waiting
    there for you?
The roses' rippling laughter, as you blushed a deeper
    red,
As though they knew your lover now had come to woo
    and wed?

Do you remember, sweetheart, how my words of passion
    burned,
And how you told me, sweetheart, that my love had
    been returned?
Do you remember, sweetheart, how you promised to
    be true,
And how my bosom bounded, sweetheart, for the love
    of you?

46

No ! you forgot the vows you made that summer night
    divine,
While I was fated to be true for evermore to mine ;
The sad September wandered through that summer's
    golden sheaves,
And scattered in her pathway palpitating withered
    leaves.

The flowers that you gave me, see, I have them still,
    my dear !
Though all have faded, sweetheart, I have kept them
    treasured here ;
Poor little withered clusters ! they have lost their old
    perfume,
And like my dead hopes, sweetheart, never more shall
    break in bloom.

The mocking-bird who trilled for us that golden sum-
    mer night
Upon a blasted tree sings through the gray November
    light ;
I listen to the gurgle of his melodies divine,
But nevermore shall feel your kisses sweetly answering
    mine.

RENAN'S LIFE OF JESUS.

WONDERFUL story of sad, sad years,
Wonderful story of toils and tears,
Annals of anguish, of grief and gloom,
Breaking at last into brilliant bloom.

Over and over again I tread
Vistas where Jesus has begged His bread,
Soothing and healing, with words of love,
Whiter than wings of a snow-white dove.

Beautiful words that silence our strife,
Beautiful words of light and of life,
Beautiful words no doom can destroy,
Beautiful words bringing dreams of joy ;

Beautiful words that shall right all wrongs,
Beautiful words like the angels' songs,
Beautiful words that have calmed my fears,
Beautiful words that have dried my tears.

Sweeter than breath of the spring-time flowers,
Softer than swirls of the autumn showers,
Splendor of song and splendor of story,
Decking His brow with garlands of glory !

48

Lighter than touch of an angel's fingers,
Clearer than notes of the stateliest singers,
Pathos of winds in the pine-trees sighing,
Sobs of a harp in the distance dying!

Dreaming of Thee, I ponder alone,
Longing for Thee, I sob and I moan,
Doubting and fearing, forever I grieve,
Crying to Thee, "O make me believe!"

After your feet have trod to each door,
After you bless the rich and the poor,
After you smile on hut and on hall,
Come unto me, the vilest of all.

When the daylight dies in twilight cold,
And the watchers come my hands to fold,
When my poor dim eyes no pathway see,
O, prince of heaven, will you think of me?

BELLINI.

WE often wonder why he died so young,
　　Before his cheeks had lost their boyhood bloom,
Before the sweetest of his songs were sung,
　　Before his spring-time blossoms found their tomb.

But when he left his home beyond the skies
　　To tread the desolated fields of earth,
The angels kissed him, gazed with tearful eyes,
　　To see him leave their blisses for our dearth;

And they had taught him sweetest songs on high,
　　The notes that seraphs trill around the throne,
Too lovely for our sullied earth and sky,
　　Where peace and rest shall nevermore be known;

And so they said, " We bid thee never sing
　　The songs we taught thee unto mortal ears;
The tidings of our joys no soul must bring
　　To still their sobs or wipe away their tears;

" Their hearts must never know our secret bliss,
　　The peerless glories of our home on high;
So if thou ever darest tread amiss,
　　Remember that thy day of doom is nigh."

But when he came, he melted at our tears,
   And sang the notes of angels in the skies,
To still our sobs and soothe our cruel fears,—
   The sweetest of our sweetest melodies.

And so the angels, jealous of our race,
   Called Death to still his grand, triumphant stave ;
They slew him in his glory and his grace,
   And hushed the sweet songs in his silent grave.

THE CRY OF A DEBTOR.

ONCE, in the glory of my morning years,
  When, like my life, the whole wide world was young,
When earth seemed free from sighs and sobs and tears,
  And love was like a lyric still unsung;

When boyish heart and soul were free from stain
  And I knew not the face of dark despair,
While still the garlands hid the iron chain,
  Before the lion leaped from out his lair;

I heeded not the world's time-worn advice,
  Which whispered that the one friend was a purse,
And so they shut me from my paradise,
  And bade me wander with a debtor's curse.

So day by day my hopes have passed away,
  Day after day I struggle to forget,
Day after day my locks are growing gray,
  And I am slaving for the monster, Debt.

I heed no more the summer or the spring,
  The autumn aster or the April bud,
The bluebird's warble or the redbird's wing,—
  I only hear a clamor for my blood.

O for the freedom of old days again !
  O for the glory of those golden skies !
O for the high ambitions that are slain !
  O for the mirth of old-time melodies !

But so my heart must cast its hopes away,
  Till rest and peace and calmness all are gone,
Like some frail ship with furious storms at bay,
  Whose men throw out her treasures one by one ;

Or like the Russian traveller in his sleigh,
  Who hears the wolves pursue with curdling cries,
Then casts his children, one by one, away,
  To stay their hunger as for life he flies.

The one I love best leaves me too, at last,
  To wander in a world of doubts and fears,
To brave alone the biting winter blast,
  Till death shall come to wipe away my tears.

But O, if I could give my life to pay
  My soul from out that desolating ban,
How I should long to give that life away,
  Then slumber in my grave,—an honest man !

NAPOLEON AND BYRON.

Two names together linked for evermore;
   Their onward march no kingdoms can retard;
Their banners flame on every sea and shore,
   Immortal chieftain and immortal bard.

Napoleon's name no longer awes the world,
   His legions long ago have shared his doom,
His stately empire in the dust is hurled,
   His high hopes buried in a hopeless tomb.

And Byron lost the fickle praise of man
   Amid the blossom of his youthful grace,
And then Death came to drag unto his den
   The classic beauty of that perfect face.

And yet they live triumphant o'er their shrouds,
   In song and story, legend and romance.
One, like an eagle, soars above the clouds,
   One, like a lion, rules the soul of France.

Sons of the mountains and the stormy sea,
   With souls of thunder, and with hearts of flame,
The czar of heroes, prince of poesy,
   The spouse of Beauty, and the King of Fame.

"BLESSED ARE THE DEAD WHO DIE IN THE LORD."

THEY are sleeping, softly sleeping,
  Free from fear and free from care,
Free from waiting and from weeping,
  Free from doubting and despair.

Year by year the spring comes shining,
  And the blue-eyed violets blow,
Then the summer sprays come twining
  Over those who rest below;

Autumn winds come calling, calling,
  Through the solemn midnight glooms,
Winter snows come falling, falling,
  At the portals of their tombs.

But they sleep in calm and quiet
  In the kind earth's ancient breast;
While the world is rife with riot,
  They are evermore at rest.

In their snowy shrouds they linger
  Till the dawning of the day
When a herald angel's finger
  Points them on their heavenly way.

55

There are those who died for duty,
  Trod the flints with bleeding feet,
Maidens in their half-blown beauty,
  Ardent youths and infants sweet.

And no sleeper there remembers
  Earthly hopes or earthly woes,
Joyous Junes or numb Novembers,
  Summer suns.or winter snows.

Then they rest in Eden's bosom,
  Haven of unending calms,
Fields of fruit and bud and blossom,
  Vernal vales with peerless palms.

Round my path dead leaves are flying
  While my soul is filled with fears,
At my feet the flowers are dying,
  And mine eyes are dim with tears ;

For my heart is ever aching,
  Dreaming of their bliss divine ;
Never will my dawn be breaking,
  Nor their rest and peace be mine.

www.ingramcontent.com/pod-product-compliance
Lightning Source LLC
Chambersburg PA
CBHW022037080426
42733CB00007B/862